# High, Higher, Highest

## Animals That Go to Great Heights

by Michael Dahl

illustrated by Brian Jensen

PICTURE WINDOW BOOKS
Minneapolis, Minnesota

Thanks to our advisers for their expertise, research, and advice:

Dr. James F. Hare, Associate Professor of Zoology
University of Manitoba
Winnipeg, Manitoba

Susan Kesselring, M.A., Literacy Educator
Rosemount-Apple Valley-Eagan (Minnesota) School District

Editorial Director: Carol Jones
Managing Editor: Catherine Neitge
Creative Director: Keith Griffin
Editor: Christianne Jones
Story Consultant: Terry Flaherty
Designer: Nathan Gassman
Production Artist: Angela Kilmer
Page Production: Picture Window Books
The illustrations in this book were created with pastels.

Picture Window Books
5115 Excelsior Boulevard, Suite 232
Minneapolis, MN 55416
877-845-8392
www.picturewindowbooks.com

Printed in the United
States of America.

Library of Congress Cataloging-in-Publication Data
Dahl, Michael.
High, higher, highest : animals that go to great heights /
written by Michael Dahl ; illustrated by Brian Jensen.
p. cm. — (Animal extremes)
Includes bibliographical references (p.     ) and index.
ISBN 1-4048-1016-1 (hardcover)
1. Animals—Miscellanea—Juvenile literature. 2.  Habitat (Ecology)—Juvenile
literature. I. Jensen, Brian. II. Title.
QL49.D3131 2005
590—dc22
2005003734

Animals live everywhere. They fly over the highest mountains and swim in the deepest oceans. They run over the hottest deserts and dive into the coldest waters.

Look up and see the extreme heights some animals can go. Watch the numbers on the number line rise as you turn each page.

Tap-tap-
tap-tap!

An acorn woodpecker taps high in
a tree in the western United States.
It's at 25 feet.

Can any animal go higher?

40 ft
(12 m)

35 ft
(11 m)

30 ft
(9 m)

25 ft
(8 m)

20 ft
(6 m)

15 ft
(5 m)

10 ft
(3 m)

5 ft
(2 m)

Yes! The howler monkey can! It's at 100 feet. It leaps across the forest canopy in southern Mexico.

6

Can any animal go higher?

160 ft
(49 m)

140 ft
(43 m)

120 ft
(37 m)

100 ft
(31 m)

80 ft
(24 m)

60 ft
(18 m)

40 ft
(12 m)

20 ft
(6 m)

Yes! The alpine grasshopper can!
It feeds on a grasses in the meadows
of the Rocky Mountains. It's at 3,200 feet.

Can any animal go higher?

4,000 ft
(.220 m)

3,500 ft
(1,068 m)

(3,200 ft.; 1,066 m)

3,000 ft
(915 m)

2,500 ft
(763 m)

2,000 ft
(610 m)

1,500 ft
(458 m)

1,000 ft
(305 m)

500 ft
(153 m)

**Yes!** The blue-winged goose can! It builds its nest at 6,000 feet in a highland marsh in Ethiopia.

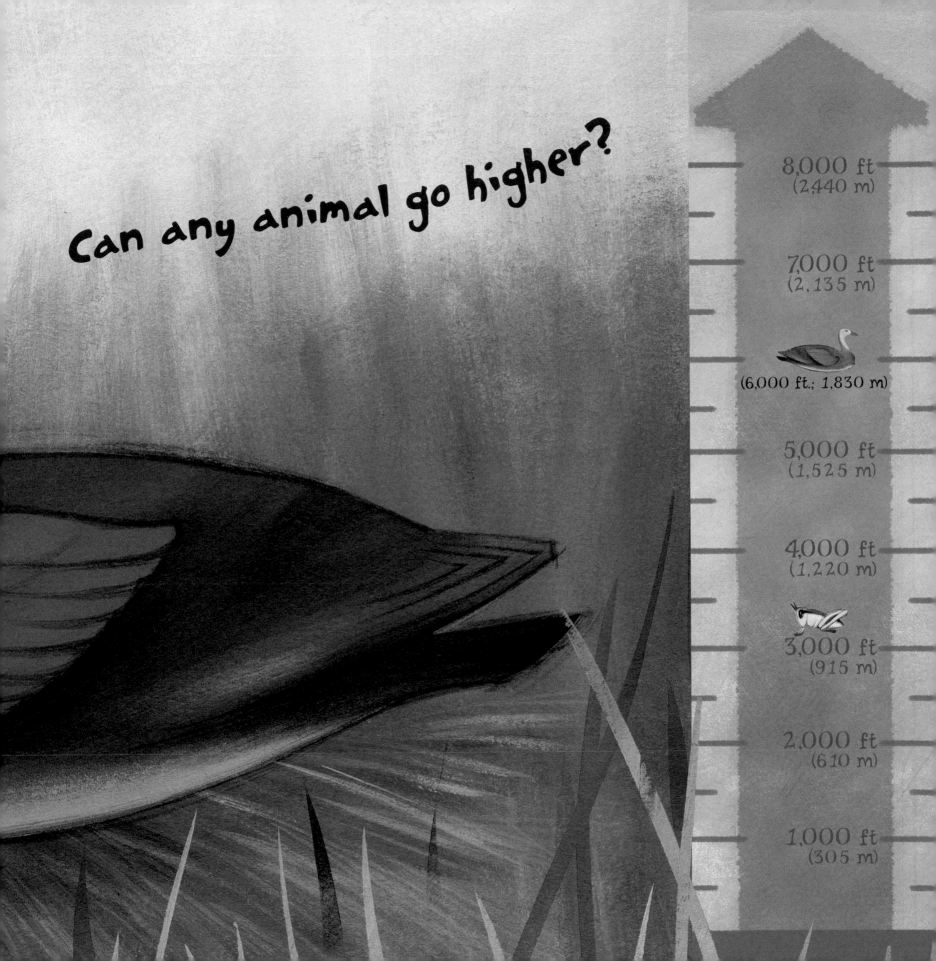

Can any animal go higher?

8,000 ft
(2,440 m)

7,000 ft
(2,135 m)

(6,000 ft.; 1,830 m)

5,000 ft
(1,525 m)

4,000 ft
(1,220 m)

3,000 ft
(915 m)

2,000 ft
(610 m)

1,000 ft
(305 m)

**Yes!** The snow leopard can!
It's at 18,000 feet. It pads silently
over the mountain snow in central Asia.

Can any animal go higher?

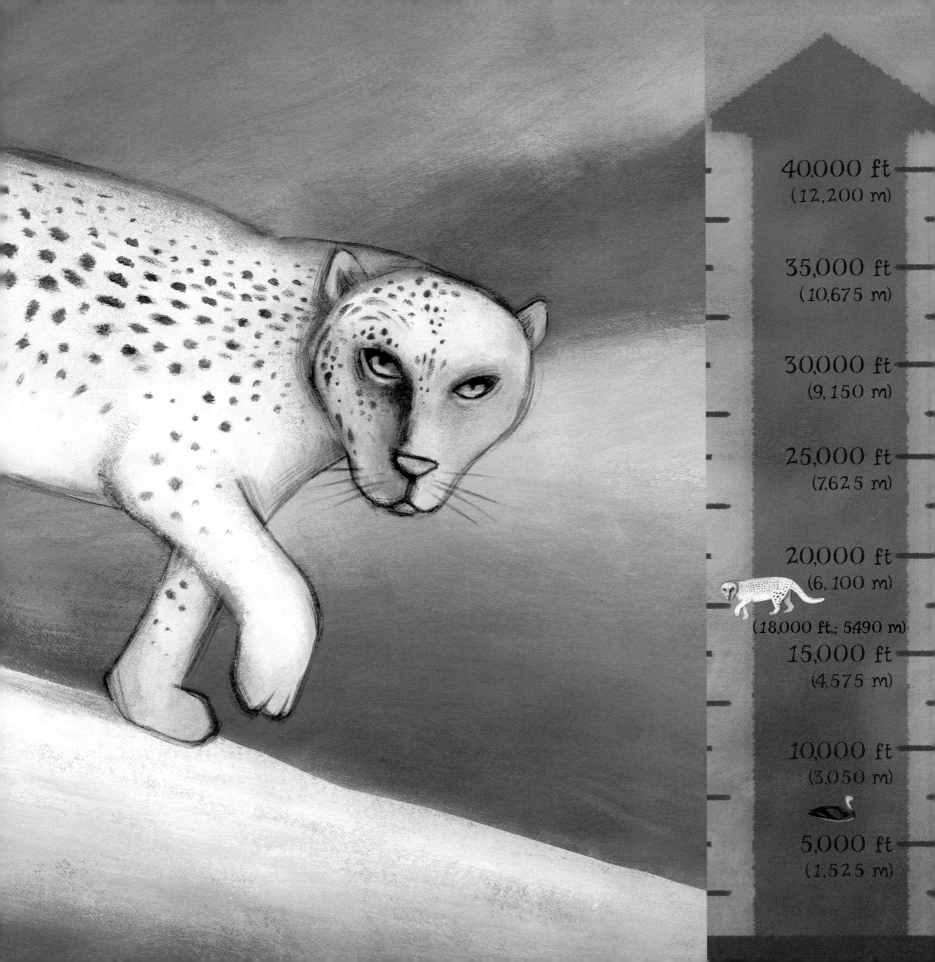

40,000 ft
(12,200 m)

35,000 ft
(10,675 m)

30,000 ft
(9,150 m)

25,000 ft
(7,625 m)

20,000 ft
(6,100 m)

(18,000 ft.; 5,490 m)

15,000 ft
(4,575 m)

10,000 ft
(3,050 m)

5,000 ft
(1,525 m)

**Yes!** The alpine chough can! It hunts for food at 24,000 feet in the Alps of southern Europe.

14

Can any animal go higher?

40,000 ft
(12,200 m)

35,000 ft
(10,675 m)

30,000 ft
(9,150 m)

25,000 ft
(7,625 m)

(24,000 ft.; 7,320 m)

20,000 ft
(6,100 m)

15,000 ft
(4,575 m)

10,000 ft
(3,050 m)

5,000 ft
(1,525 m)

**Yes!** A bar-headed goose can! It soars at 29,000 feet with its flock above the snow-capped peaks of Mount Everest.

Can any animal go higher?

40,000 ft
(12,200 m)

35,000 ft
(10,675 m)

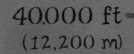
30,000 ft
(9,150 m)
(29,000 ft.; 8,845 m)

25,000 ft
(7,625 m)

20,000 ft
(6,100 m)

15,000 ft
(4,575 m)

10,000 ft
(3,050 m)

5,000 ft
(1,525 m)

**Yes!** A griffin vulture can! It peers through the clouds over the African savanna. It's at 37,900 feet.

Can any animal go higher?

40,000 ft
(12,200 m)
(37,900 ft.; 11,560 m)

35,000 ft
(10,675 m)

30,000 ft
(9,100 m)

25,000 ft
(7,625 m)

20,000 ft
(6,100 m)

15,000 ft
(4,575 m)

10,000 ft
(3,050 m)

5,000 ft
(1,525 m)

# Extreme
# Fun Facts

The Ruppell's griffin vulture is the world's highest-flying bird. It was seen flying at 37,900 feet (11, 560 meters).

The bar-headed goose gets its name from the two black bars, or stripes, on its white head.

The yellow-billed chough builds its nest higher than all other birds. This bird is also called the alpine chough.

A snow leopard has extra fur on the bottom of its paws for protection against the snow and the cold.

The blue-winged goose often rests its neck on its back. This habit makes the goose easy to identify.

griffin vulture

bar-headed goose

alpine chough

snow leopard

blue-winged goose

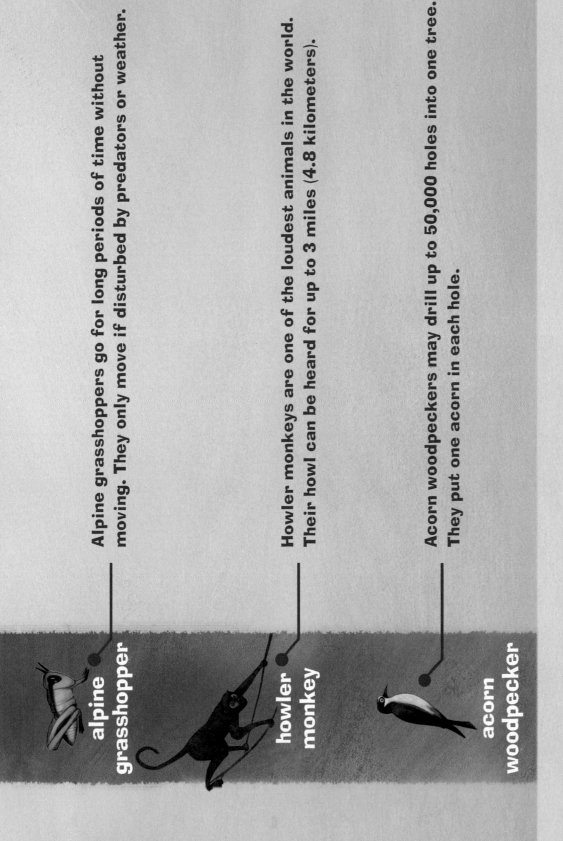

**alpine grasshopper** — Alpine grasshoppers go for long periods of time without moving. They only move if disturbed by predators or weather.

**howler monkey** — Howler monkeys are one of the loudest animals in the world. Their howl can be heard for up to 3 miles (4.8 kilometers).

**acorn woodpecker** — Acorn woodpeckers may drill up to 50,000 holes into one tree. They put one acorn in each hole.

# Glossary

**canopy**—the middle layer of the rain forest where the greenery is thick and there is little sunlight

**highland**—high or hilly lands

**marsh**—a wetland that is covered with water for most of the year and has no trees

**migrate**—to travel from one area to another

**predator**—an animal that hunts and eats other animals

**savanna**—flat, grassy plain that has only a few trees

**soar**—to fly high in the air

# To Learn More

## At the Library

Galko, Francine. *Mountain Animals.* Chicago: Heinemann Library, 2003.

Taylor, Barbara. *Birds and Other Flying Animals.* Columbus, Ohio: Peter Bedrick Books, 2003.

Winnie, John. *Highlife: Animals of the Alpine World.* Flagstaff, Ariz.: Northland Pub., 1996.

## On the Web

FactHound offers a safe, fun way to find Web sites related to this book. All of the sites on FactHound have been researched by our staff. *www.facthound.com*

1.  Visit the FactHound home page.

2.  Enter a search word related to this book, or type in this special code: 1404810161

3.  Click on the FETCH IT button.

Your trusty FactHound will fetch the best sites for you!

## Index

# Look for all of the books in the Animal Extremes series:

**Cold, Colder, Coldest:** *Animals That Adapt to Cold Weather*

**Deep, Deeper, Deepest:** *Animals That Go to Great Depths*

**Fast, Faster, Fastest:** *Animals That Move at Great Speeds*

**High, Higher, Highest:** *Animals That Go to Great Heights*

**Hot, Hotter, Hottest:** *Animals That Adapt to Great Heat*

**Old, Older, Oldest:** *Animals That Live Long Lives*